HOLIDAY
COCKTAILS

Holiday Cocktails

13-Digit ISBN: 978-1-64643-174-8
10-Digit ISBN: 1-64643-174-X

This book may be ordered by mail from the publisher. Please include $5.99 for postage and handling. Please support your local bookseller first!

Books published by Cider Mill Press Book Publishers are available at special discounts for bulk purchases in the United States by corporations, institutions, and other organizations. For more information, please contact the publisher.

Cider Mill Press Book Publishers
"Where good books are ready for press"
PO Box 454
12 Spring Street
Kennebunkport, Maine 04046
Visit us online!
cidermillpress.com

Typography: Operetta 12 and Sofia Pro
Photos on 34, 37, 57, 109, 178, 189, and 227 courtesy of Cider Mill Press.
All other photos used under official license from Shutterstock.com.

Front Cover Image: Gath'ring Winter Fuel, see page 76

Printed in China
1 2 3 4 5 6 7 8 9 0
First Edition

HOLIDAY COCKTAILS

OVER **100** SIMPLE COCKTAILS TO CELEBRATE THE SEASON

CIDER MILL PRESS

BOOK PUBLISHERS
KENNEBUNKPORT, MAINE

CONTENTS

INTRODUCTION

The holidays are indeed the most wonderful time of the year. Through some magical means, the dynamism of the season provides us with a much-needed nudge toward being the kind of people we should be. Suddenly, it's easy to put others before ourselves, to find time to visit with those who matter, to step back and take a moment to both look back and orient ourselves toward the future, rededicate ourselves to the lives we want.

It's also a time when there's plenty to celebrate. Or, rather, the one time we allow ourselves to recognize how much there is to celebrate, and accept it. As the temperatures plunge and the available daylight begins to be severely truncated, we find ourselves craving company and exuberance, and are lucky to find others in the same boat.

This book is an acknowledgment of our festive inclinations once the calendar hits mid-November, as well as the various forms these proclivities take. Yes, the holidays are the time we come together, but it also recognizes that during the course of the season, there will be slight shifts in what we require.

For those who throw the big party on the block, there's a host of inventive punches and batch cocktails that will lighten your load, and make sure everyone has a good time getting on the same page. On those snowy days when all you want to do is sit before the fire with a loved one and either calm the nerves frayed by commuting over slick roads, or get rid the chills picked up while shoveling, there's a series of warming toddies that will serve as the ideal tonic. When an old friend stops by unexpectedly and asks for their all-time favorite serve, you'll find a section of classic recipes that will keep the good vibes rolling along. There's an array of sparkling cocktails for those moments when the excitement peaks and only the thrilling effervescence of bubbles seems fit. And, when your spirits are flagging slightly and the breakneck pace of the season has you feeling run down, there's a series of spirit-reviving cocktails that will keep you in mind of the magic of the holidays, that combination of joy, hope, and giving that have birthed so many memories, movies, and memorable tunes.

PARTY
PROVISIONS

The big, festive groups of people, community spirit, and air of generosity that circulate around the holidays lend themselves to punches and batch cocktails. From traditional rum punches to bold eggnogs and inventive sangrias that will entice even the most staid and conservative folks, you'll have no issue finding a centerpiece for your next holiday party.

ALL MY
FRIENDS

SUGAR, FOR THE RIMS (OPTIONAL)

1½ CUPS GRAND MARNIER

3 (750 ML) BOTTLES OF CHAMPAGNE

3 CUPS FRESH ORANGE JUICE

1. If using the sugar, pour ¼ cup of the Grand Marnier into a bowl. Dip the rims of the champagne flutes into the liqueur and then coat them with the sugar.

2. Place the remaining orange liqueur, Champagne, and orange juice in a large punch bowl, stir gently, and pour into the rimmed glasses.

HOT APPLE CIDER

6 CUPS APPLE CIDER

3 CUPS BOURBON

5 CINNAMON STICKS

3 ORANGE PEELS, FOR GARNISH

30 TO 40 WHOLE CLOVES, FOR GARNISH

1. Place the apple cider, bourbon, and cinnamon sticks in a slow cooker and cook on low for 2 hours, making sure the mixture does not come to a boil.

2. Cut the orange peels into rectangles and press the cloves into them. Garnish each glass with a clove-studded orange peel.

CAFÉ
MOCHA

8 CUPS WHOLE MILK

1 CUP HEAVY CREAM

½ CUP SUGAR, PLUS MORE TO TASTE

½ CUP FRESHLY BREWED ESPRESSO

8 OZ. BITTERSWEET CHOCOLATE, CHOPPED

1 CUP AGED RUM

1 TABLESPOON ORANGE ZEST

½ TEASPOON FINE SEA SALT

1. Place the milk, cream, sugar, and espresso in a saucepan and warm it over medium heat.

2. Place the chocolate in a bowl. When the milk mixture is hot, ladle 1 cup of it over the chocolate and whisk until the chocolate is completely melted, adding more of the warm milk mixture if the melted chocolate mixture is too thick.

3. Pour the melted chocolate mixture into the pot of warm milk and whisk to combine. Add the rum, orange zest, and salt and stir to combine. Pour into mugs and enjoy.

PLANTER'S PUNCH

3 CUPS LIGHT RUM

1½ CUPS DARK RUM

1 OZ. ANGOSTURA BITTERS

3 CUPS ORANGE JUICE

½ CUP PINEAPPLE JUICE

1 CUP TRIPLE SEC

2 OZ. GRENADINE

ORANGE SLICES, FOR GARNISH

1. Place all of the ingredients, except for the orange slices, in a large punch bowl, add blocks of ice, and stir to combine.

2. Serve over ice in Collins glasses and garnish with orange slices.

AT THE MERCY OF INERTIA

3 CUPS BOURBON

1 CUP WHOLE MILK

1 OZ. SIMPLE SYRUP (SEE BELOW)

1 TEASPOON PURE VANILLA EXTRACT

FRESHLY GRATED NUTMEG, FOR GARNISH

1. Place all of the ingredients, except for the nutmeg, in a large punch bowl, add large blocks of ice, and stir to combine.

2. Garnish with the nutmeg and serve in coupes or rocks glasses.

Simple Syrup

Named due to its humble components—equal parts sugar and water—and the ease of making it—just place the sugar (or honey) and water in a saucepan, stir as it comes to a boil in order to help the sugar dissolve, and then let it cool—there is nothing basic about the role simple syrup plays in cocktail making. Whether it is there to offset the lemon or lime juice, allow a tucked-away flavor to surface, or add body and viscosity to a drink, simple syrup definitively transcends its modest construction.

WHEN
I COME
KNOCKING

2 CUPS RUM

2 CUPS CROWN ROYAL WHISKEY

2 CUPS BRANDY

½ OZ. GRENADINE

MARASCHINO CHERRIES,
FOR GARNISH

1. Place all of the ingredients, except for the maraschino cherries, in a large punch bowl, add blocks of ice, and stir to combine.

2. Serve over ice in rocks glasses and garnish with the maraschino cherries.

IT'S A BETTER THAN GOOD TIME

2 CUPS AGED RUM

1 CUP BOURBON

1 CUP SIMPLE SYRUP

2 CUPS HEAVY CREAM

FRESHLY GRATED NUTMEG,
FOR GARNISH

1. Place all of the ingredients, except for the nutmeg, in a large punch bowl, add large blocks of ice, and stir to combine.

2. Garnish with the nutmeg and serve in coupes or over ice in rocks glasses.

WHISKEY STORY TIME

1 (750 ML) BOTTLE OF BOURBON

6 CUPS ORANGE JUICE

2 CUPS FRESH LEMON JUICE

¼ OZ. BLOOD ORANGE BITTERS

½ CUP SIMPLE SYRUP

MARASCHINO CHERRIES, FOR GARNISH

1. Place all of the ingredients, except for the maraschino cherries, in a large punch bowl, add large blocks of ice, and stir until chilled.

2. Serve over ice in Collins glasses and garnish with maraschino cherries.

AFTER THE
GOLDRUSH

6 LEMONS

1 CUP SUGAR

8 BAGS OF CHAI TEA

4 CUPS BOILING WATER

1 CUP BOURBON

1 (12 OZ.) BOTTLE OF GINGER BEER

LEMON WHEELS, FOR GARNISH

CINNAMON STICKS, FOR GARNISH

WHOLE CLOVES, FOR GARNISH

STAR ANISE PODS, FOR GARNISH

ALLSPICE BERRIES, FOR GARNISH

1. Peel the lemons and set the fruit aside. Place the lemon peels and the sugar in a bowl, muddle, and let stand for 1 hour. Juice the lemons and strain to remove all pulp.

2. Place the tea bags in the boiling water and steep for 5 minutes. Remove the tea bags and discard. Add the sugar-and-lemon peel mixture to the tea and stir until the sugar has dissolved. Strain and discard the solids.

3. Add the bourbon and the lemon juice, stir to combine, and chill the punch in the refrigerator for 1 hour.

4. Add ginger beer and large blocks of ice just before serving. Gently stir to combine, serve over ice in rocks glasses, and garnish with lemon wheels, cinnamon sticks, cloves, star anise pods, and allspice berries.

COZY
CABIN

4 PEARS

2 CUPS FRESH LEMON JUICE

½ OZ. ROSEMARY SYRUP
(SEE BELOW)

4 CUPS SCOTCH WHISKY

1½ CUPS GRAND MARNIER

SPRIGS OF FRESH ROSEMARY,
TORCHED, FOR GARNISH

1. Place the pears, lemon juice, and syrup in a mixing bowl and muddle.

2. Transfer the mixture to a large punch bowl, add large blocks of ice, the Scotch whisky, and Grand Marnier, and stir to combine.

3. Serve over ice in rocks glasses and garnish with sprigs of torched rosemary.

Rosemary Syrup

Place 1 cup sugar and 1 cup water in a small saucepan and bring to a boil over medium heat, stirring to dissolve the sugar. Add 3 sprigs of fresh rosemary, remove the pan from heat, and let the syrup cool completely. Strain before using.

MEET ME IN ST. LOUIS

2 CUPS DOMAINE DE CANTON
GINGER LIQUEUR

1½ CUPS BOURBON

1½ CUPS AMONTILLADO SHERRY

2 CUPS BREWED BLACK TEA,
COOLED TO ROOM TEMPERATURE

2 CUPS GINGER BEER

2 CUPS FRESH LEMON JUICE

1¼ CUPS OLEO SACCHARUM
(SEE BELOW)

1. Place all of the ingredients in a large punch bowl, add blocks of ice, and stir until chilled.

2. Serve over ice in Collins glasses.

Oleo Saccharum

Place the peels of 8 lemons and 2 oranges and 2½ cups sugar in a large bowl and toss to combine. Using some serious elbow grease, use a muddler or the back of a heavy wooden spoon to mash the peels until they express all of their oil. Let the mixture macerate for 30 minutes to 1 hour. Strain the liquid and discard the peels.

NORTHERN LIGHTS

3 CUPS GIN

1½ CUPS LILLET ROSE

1 CUP ORANGE LIQUEUR

2 CUPS FRESH GRAPEFRUIT JUICE

½ CUP FRESH LIME JUICE

GRAPEFRUIT TWISTS, FOR GARNISH

1. Place all of the ingredients, except for the grapefruit twists, in a large punch bowl, add large blocks of ice, and stir until chilled.

2. Serve in coupes or over ice in rocks glasses and garnish with the grapefruit twists.

LET IT
SNOW

2 CUPS ABSINTHE

1 CUP HERBSAINT

1 CUP WHITE CRÈME DE MENTHE

2 CUPS HEAVY CREAM

¼ OZ. SIMPLE SYRUP

DASH OF ORANGE BLOSSOM WATER

1 EGG WHITE

FRESH MINT, FOR GARNISH

1. Place all of the ingredients, except for the mint, in a blender and puree until combined.

2. Place the mixture in a large punch bowl, add large blocks of ice, and stir until chilled.

3. Serve in coupes or over ice in rocks glasses and garnish with fresh mint.

CLASSIC
RED
SANGRIA

2 (750 ML) BOTTLES OF RED WINE

1½ CUPS BRANDY

½ CUP SIMPLE SYRUP

1 CUP ORANGE JUICE

2 APPLES, CORED, SEEDED, AND DICED

2 ORANGES, PEELED AND SLICED THIN

5 LEMON WHEELS

5 LIME WHEELS

1. Place all of the ingredients into a large, airtight container and seal.

2. Refrigerate for 24 hours to allow the flavors to combine and pour the sangria into a punch bowl when ready to serve.

IN A
PEAR
TREE

2 (750 ML) BOTTLES OF DRY RED WINE

4 PEARS, CORED, SEEDED, AND DICED

3 CUPS SEEDLESS GRAPES, FROZEN

3 CUPS ORANGE JUICE

1 (12 OZ.) CAN OF CREAM SODA

1. Place all of the ingredients, except for the soda, in a large pitcher or punch bowl. Cover and refrigerate for 4 or more hours.

2. When ready to serve, add large blocks of ice and the soda and gently stir. Serve in wine glasses or champagne flutes.

DANCE OF TWINKLE AND SHADOW

2 (750 ML) BOTTLES OF DRY RED WINE

2 PLUMS, PITTED, SLICED THIN, AND FROZEN

1 CUP CHERRIES, PITTED AND HALVED

1 CUP BLACKBERRIES

½ CUP GRAND MARNIER

4 CUPS SELTZER WATER

1. Place all of the ingredients, except for the seltzer water, in a large pitcher or punch bowl. Cover and refrigerate for 4 or more hours.

2. When ready to serve, add large blocks of ice and the seltzer and gently stir to combine. Serve in wine glasses or champagne flutes.

COZY
CHRISTMAS

2 (750 ML) BOTTLES OF DRY RED WINE

4 APPLES, CORED, SEEDED, AND DICED

2 ORANGES, SLICED THIN

½ CUP QUALITY APPLE VODKA

2 CUPS APPLE CIDER

DASH OF CINNAMON

POMEGRANATE SEEDS, FOR GARNISH

1. Place all of the ingredients, except for the pomegranate seeds, in a large pitcher or punch bowl. Cover and refrigerate for 4 or more hours.

2. Serve over ice in wine glasses and garnish with the pomegranate seeds.

BRING US SOME FIGGY PUDDING

2 (750 ML) BOTTLES OF DRY RED WINE

2 CUPS FRESH RASPBERRIES

6 FIGS, DICED AND FROZEN

2 CUPS FIG JUICE

1 CUP POMEGRANATE JUICE

2 CUPS SELTZER WATER

SPRIGS OF FRESH THYME, FOR GARNISH

1. Place all of the ingredients, except for the seltzer and thyme, in a large pitcher or punch bowl. Cover and refrigerate for 4 or more hours.

2. When ready to serve, add the seltzer water and gently stir. Serve over ice and garnish each with a sprig of thyme.

SLEIGH RIDE

2 (750 ML) BOTTLES OF DRY WHITE WINE

2 CUPS SEEDLESS RED GRAPES, HALVED AND FROZEN

4 PLUMS, PITTED, DICED, AND FROZEN

¾ CUP GINGER SYRUP (SEE BELOW)

2 CUPS SELTZER WATER

1. Place all of the ingredients, except for the seltzer water, in a large pitcher or punch bowl. Cover and refrigerate for 4 or more hours.

2. When ready to serve, add the seltzer and gently stir. Serve over ice in wine glasses.

Ginger Syrup

Place 1 cup sugar and 1 cup water in a saucepan and bring to a boil, stirring to dissolve the sugar. Remove the pan from heat, stir in ¼ cup of peeled and thinly sliced fresh ginger, and let the mixture steep for 2 hours. Strain before using.

OLD
FEZZIWIG

1 CUP FRESH LEMON JUICE

½ CUP GIN

24 BLACKBERRIES

12 RASPBERRIES

2 (750 ML) BOTTLES OF SPARKLING
WINE, VERY COLD

1. Place the lemon juice and gin in a pitcher and stir to combine.

2. Divide this mixture and the berries between wine glasses or champagne flutes and top with the sparkling wine.

APRÈS
EVERYTHING

4 CUPS FROZEN RASPBERRIES

2 CUPS FROZEN BLUEBERRIES

1 CUP LAVENDER SYRUP (SEE BELOW)

2 (750 ML) BOTTLES OF WHITE WINE, VERY COLD

FRESH MINT, FOR GARNISH

1. Place the raspberries, blueberries, and syrup in a large pitcher or punch bowl, stir to combine, cover, and refrigerate for 1 hour.

2. Divide the mixture between wine glasses or champagne flutes and top with the wine. Garnish with fresh mint.

Lavender Syrup

Place 1 cup water and 1 cup sugar in a saucepan and bring to a boil, stirring to dissolve the sugar. Stir in 2 tablespoons of dried lavender, remove the pan from heat, and let the syrup cool. Strain before using.

OLD
SCHOOL
CHRISTMAS

2 NAVEL ORANGES, SLICED THIN

¼ CUP FRESH LEMON JUICE

½ CUP GRAND MARNIER

12 RASPBERRIES

2 (750 ML) BOTTLES OF SPARKLING
WINE, VERY COLD

1. Reserve six slices of orange and place the rest in a bowl.

2. Add the lemon juice and Grand Marnier, stir to combine, cover, and refrigerate for 1 hour.

3. Divide this mixture, the reserved orange slices, and the raspberries between wine glasses or champagne flutes and top with the sparkling wine.

LAST
CHRISTMAS

4½ CUPS WHOLE MILK

1½ CUPS HALF-AND-HALF

3 CUPS BRANDY

1½ CUPS SIMPLE SYRUP

2 TABLESPOONS PURE VANILLA
EXTRACT

FRESHLY GRATED NUTMEG,
FOR GARNISH

1. Place all of the ingredients, except for the
   nutmeg, in a punch bowl, add large blocks of
   ice, and stir until chilled.

2. Garnish with the nutmeg and serve over ice in
   Nick & Nora glasses or coupes.

NIPPING
AT YOUR
NOSE

3 CUPS FRESH LEMON JUICE

2 CUPS COGNAC

1 CUP SIMPLE SYRUP

¼ CUP ORANGE LIQUEUR

3 CUPS PORT WINE

LEMON WEDGES, FOR GARNISH

1. Place the lemon juice, Cognac, simple syrup, orange liqueur, and Port in a punch bowl, add large blocks of ice, and stir until chilled.

2. Serve in coupes or over ice in Collins glasses and garnish with lemon wedges.

ON
DONNER

3 CUPS APPLEJACK

1½ CUPS BÉNÉDICTINE

2 OZ. DOLIN BLANC

2 CUPS APPLE JUICE

1 CUP CLUB SODA

1. Place the applejack, Bénédictine, Dolin Blanc, apple juice, and club soda in a large punch bowl, add large blocks of ice, and stir until chilled.

2. Add the club soda, gently stir, and serve over ice in Collins glasses.

MS. CLAUS'S CIDER

3 CUPS SPICED RUM

½ CUP APPLE SCHNAPPS

1½ CUPS CINNAMON SCHNAPPS

1 CUP LEMON–LIME SELTZER

FRESH MINT, FOR GARNISH

1. Place the rum and schnapps in a large punch bowl, add large blocks of ice, and stir until chilled.

2. Add the seltzer and stir gently to combine.

3. Serve over ice in rocks glasses and garnish with fresh mint.

THE
EPIPHANY

3 CUPS ABSOLUT CITRON

1½ CUPS TRIPLE SEC

1½ CUPS WHITE CRANBERRY JUICE

½ CUP FRESH LIME JUICE

1½ CUPS LEMON–LIME SELTZER

FRESH MINT, FOR GARNISH

1. Place the vodka, triple sec, and white cranberry juice in a large punch bowl, add large blocks of ice, and stir until chilled.

2. Add the seltzer and stir gently to combine.

3. Serve over ice in rocks glasses and garnish with fresh mint.

CLASSIC EGGNOG

6 EGGS, BEATEN UNTIL FROTHY

½ TEASPOON PURE VANILLA EXTRACT

¼ TEASPOON FRESHLY GRATED
NUTMEG, PLUS MORE FOR GARNISH

1 CUP SUGAR, PLUS 1 TABLESPOON

¾ CUP BRANDY

⅓ CUP DARK RUM

2 CUPS HEAVY CREAM

2 CUPS MILK

CINNAMON STICKS, FOR GARNISH

1. Place all of the ingredients in a large punch bowl and whisk to combine.

2. Chill in the refrigerator until ready to serve, garnishing each glass with additional nutmeg and cinnamon sticks.

COFFEE
EGGNOG

2½ OZ. SIMPLE SYRUP

2 CUPS SCOTCH WHISKY

1 CUP KAHLÚA

4 CUPS MILK

2 CUPS HALF-AND-HALF

3 TABLESPOONS INSTANT COFFEE

6 EGGS

2 CUPS ICE

CINNAMON, FOR GARNISH

1. Place all of the ingredients, except for the cinnamon, in a large mixing bowl and stir to combine.

2. Working in batches, add the mixture to a blender and puree until smooth.

3. Serve over ice in rocks glasses and garnish each drink with cinnamon.

BALTIMORE
EGGNOG

12 EGGS, YOLKS AND WHITES
SEPARATED

2 CUPS CASTER SUGAR

2 CUPS COGNAC

1 CUP DARK RUM

1 CUP MADEIRA

6 CUPS MILK

2 CUPS HEAVY CREAM

FRESHLY GRATED NUTMEG,
FOR GARNISH

1. Place the egg yolks and sugar in a bowl and beat until the mixture is pale and thick.

2. Stir in the Cognac, rum, Madeira, milk, and cream. Refrigerate until thoroughly chilled.

3. When ready to serve, beat the egg whites until they hold stiff peaks. Transfer the chilled base to a large, chilled punch bowl and then fold in the beaten egg whites. Do not stir.

4. Serve in cocktail glasses or rocks glasses and garnish with nutmeg.

VIN
CHAUD

2 (750 ML) BOTTLES OF RED WINE

2 STAR ANISE PODS

2-INCH PIECE OF FRESH GINGER

5 WHOLE CLOVES

3 CARDAMOM PODS

2 TABLESPOONS ORANGE ZEST

2 TABLESPOONS LEMON ZEST

¾ CUP HONEY

¾ CUP COGNAC

CINNAMON STICKS, FOR GARNISH

ORANGE SLICES, FOR GARNISH

1. Place all of the ingredients, except for the Cognac and garnishes, in a saucepan and bring to a simmer over medium heat.

2. Remove from heat and stir in the Cognac.

3. Pour into warmed mugs and garnish with cinnamon sticks and orange slices.

If you'd prefer something other than Cognac, Calvados is a solid alternative.

FLAMING HOT GOOSE

6 CUPS PEAR CIDER

1 (375 ML) BOTTLE OF BRANDY

¾ CUP AGED RUM

2 (12 OZ.) BOTTLES OF SPICY GINGER BEER

⅓ CUP SPICED SYRUP (SEE BELOW)

2 DASHES OF PEYCHAUD'S BITTERS

PEAR SLICES, FOR GARNISH

LEMON WHEELS, FOR GARNISH

1. Place all of the ingredients, except for the garnishes, in a large punch bowl, add large blocks of ice, and stir until chilled.

2. Serve over ice in rocks glasses and garnish with the pear slices and lemon wheels.

Spiced Syrup

In a small saucepan, combine 1 cup water, 1 cup pomegranate juice, 3 cinnamon sticks, 5 whole cloves, 5 allspice berries, and 3 cardamom pods. Cook over low heat, stirring frequently, until the sugar has dissolved. Remove from heat, let the syrup cool, and strain before using.

GATH'RING WINTER FUEL

1 (375 ML) BOTTLE OF AGED RUM OR COGNAC

¾ CUP ORANGE LIQUEUR

¼ CUP SPICED HIBISCUS SYRUP (SEE BELOW)

3 DASHES OF PEYCHAUD'S BITTERS

2 (750 ML) BOTTLES OF SPARKLING WINE

CRANBERRIES, FOR GARNISH

1. Place all of the ingredients, except for the sparkling wine and cranberries, in a large punch bowl, add large blocks of ice, and stir until chilled.

2. Add the sparkling wine and gently stir to combine.

3. Serve in wine glasses or champagne flutes and garnish with cranberries.

Spiced Hibiscus Syrup

Place 1 cup water, ½ cup dried hibiscus blossoms (or 6 bags of hibiscus tea), 1 cinnamon stick, 5 whole cloves, 5 allspice berries, and 1 split vanilla bean pod in a small saucepan and bring to boil over medium heat. Remove from heat and let the mixture steep for 15 to 20 minutes. Strain, discard the solids, and return the liquid to the pan. Bring to a boil over medium heat and add ¾ cup demerara sugar. Stir until the sugar has dissolved, remove from heat, and let cool before using.

WINTER
WARMERS

As magical and joyous as the holidays are, we all have a tendency to get caught up in the tremendous energy of the season, and then run down by it. Add in the dwindling sunlight and plummeting temperatures, and it's easy for a bit of a chill to enter your spirit, and your tone. These comforting cocktails guarantee that both retain their warmth.

HOT
TODDY

2 OZ. BLENDED SCOTCH WHISKY

½ OZ. FRESH LEMON JUICE

¼ OZ. SIMPLE SYRUP

BOILING WATER, TO TOP

1 LEMON WEDGE, FOR GARNISH

1 CINNAMON STICK, FOR GARNISH

1. Place the Scotch, lemon juice, syrup, and water in a mug or Irish Coffee glass and stir to combine.

2. Garnish with the lemon wedge and the cinnamon stick.

HOT
BUTTERED
RUM

1 SMALL PAT OF BUTTER

1 TEASPOON BROWN SUGAR

DASH OF CINNAMON, PLUS MORE
TO TASTE

DASH OF FRESHLY GRATED NUTMEG,
PLUS MORE TO TASTE

DASH OF ORANGE ZEST, PLUS MORE
TO TASTE

SPLASH OF PURE VANILLA EXTRACT

6 OZ. BOILING WATER

2 OZ. AGED RUM

1 CINNAMON STICK, FOR GARNISH

1. Place the butter, brown sugar, cinnamon, nutmeg, and orange zest in the bottom of a mug and stir to combine.

2. Add the vanilla extract, water, and rum and stir to combine.

3. Adjust to taste and garnish with the cinnamon stick.

SKATING

2 OZ. APPLEJACK

1 TEASPOON MAPLE SYRUP

6 OZ. FRESHLY BREWED CINNAMON
APPLE TEA

1 LEMON TWIST, FOR GARNISH

4 WHOLE CLOVES, FOR GARNISH

1. Place the applejack, maple syrup, and tea in a mug and stir to combine.

2. Garnish with the lemon twist and whole cloves.

RUM
CHOCOLATE

8 OZ. MILK

1 OZ. QUALITY CHOCOLATE

1 OZ. AGED RUM

HANDFUL OF MINIATURE
MARSHMALLOWS

1. Place the milk in a small saucepan and warm it over medium-low heat until it just starts to simmer.

2. Place the chocolate in a mug, pour the warmed milk on top, and stir until smooth.

3. Stir in the rum, top with the marshmallows, and enjoy.

TOM
& JERRY

1 OZ. SIMPLE SYRUP

1 OZ. DARK RUM

1 OZ. BRANDY

2 OZ. EGGNOG, WARMED

1 CINNAMON STICK, FOR GARNISH

1. Place the syrup, rum, brandy, and eggnog in a mug or Irish coffee glass and stir to combine.

2. Garnish with the cinnamon stick.

HOT
BUTTERED
BOURBON

1 SMALL PAT OF BUTTER

1 TEASPOON BROWN SUGAR

DASH OF CINNAMON

DASH OF FRESHLY GRATED NUTMEG

PINCH OF KOSHER SALT

1½ OZ. BOURBON

DASH OF ANGOSTURA BITTERS

6 OZ. BOILING WATER

1 CINNAMON STICK, FOR GARNISH

1. Place the butter, brown sugar, cinnamon, nutmeg, salt, bourbon, and bitters in a mug and stir to combine.

2. Pour the boiling water on top, stir to combine, and garnish with the cinnamon stick.

A STRANGER IN THE ALPS

2 OZ. GIN

1 OZ. SIMPLE SYRUP

JUICE OF ½ LEMON

6 OZ. FRESHLY BREWED MINT TEA

1 PEPPERMINT STICK, FOR GARNISH

1 LEMON SLICE, FOR GARNISH

1. Place the gin, syrup, and lemon juice in a mug and stir to combine.

2. Add the tea, stir to combine, and garnish with the peppermint stick and slice of lemon.

THE
SNOWQUEEN

1 BAG OF ENGLISH BREAKFAST TEA

1 BAG OF EARL GREY TEA

6 OZ. VERY HOT WATER (170°F)

¼ OZ. SIMPLE SYRUP

1¼ OZ. HENDRICK'S GIN

DOLLOP OF WHIPPED CREAM

1. Place the tea bags and the hot water in a mug and steep for 3 minutes.

2. Stir in the simple syrup and gin, top with the whipped cream, and enjoy.

GIRL FROM THE NORTH COUNTRY

1 OZ. SCOTCH WHISKY

2 OZ. KAHLÚA

2 OZ. CRÈME DE CACAO

1 OZ. FRESHLY BREWED ESPRESSO
OR STRONG COFFEE

4 OZ. CRÈME FRAÎCHE

1. Place all of the ingredients, except for the crème fraîche, in a mug and stir to combine.

2. Layer the crème fraîche on top and enjoy.

SUGAR
FOR THE
PILL

8 OZ. WATER

2 OZ. SUGAR

6 LARGE LEMON VERBENA LEAVES,
PLUS MORE FOR GARNISH

1¼ OZ. GIN

½ OZ. FRESH KEY LIME JUICE

¼ OZ. SAFFRON SYRUP (SEE BELOW)

1. Place the water and sugar in a small saucepan and bring to a boil. Add the lemon verbena leaves, remove the pan from heat, and let steep for 5 minutes.

2. Strain into a mug, add the gin, key lime juice, and syrup, and stir to combine.

3. Garnish with the additional lemon verbena leaf and enjoy.

Saffron Syrup

Place 1 cup water and 1 cup sugar in a small saucepan and bring to a boil. Stir in ⅛ teaspoon saffron threads, remove the pan from heat, and let cool completely. Strain before using.

LAND OF
MILK
& HONEY

2 OZ. SINGLE-MALT SCOTCH WHISKY

5 OZ. FRESHLY BREWED CHAI TEA

½ OZ. MILK

½ TABLESPOON HONEY

1 CINNAMON STICK, FOR GARNISH

1 STAR ANISE POD, FOR GARNISH

1. Place the whisky, tea, milk, and honey in a mug and stir to combine.

2. Garnish with the cinnamon stick and star anise and enjoy.

A HEART
SO WHITE

1½ OZ. IRISH WHISKEY

3 OZ. HOT APPLE CIDER

½ OZ. EARL GREY SYRUP (SEE BELOW)

½ OZ. FRESH LEMON JUICE

SPLASH OF HOT WATER

2 OZ. SPARKLING WINE

1 LEMON TWIST, FOR GARNISH

1. Place the whiskey, cider, syrup, and lemon juice in a mug and stir to combine.

2. Add the splash of hot water, stir, and top with the sparkling wine.

3. Garnish with the lemon twist and enjoy.

Earl Grey Syrup

Place 1 cup water and 1 cup sugar in a small saucepan and bring to a boil, stirring to dissolve the sugar. Add 3 teabags of Earl Grey tea, remove the pan from heat, and let the syrup cool completely. Remove the tea bags before using.

IRISH
COFFEE

½ CUP FRESHLY BREWED COFFEE

DASH OF SUGAR

1 OZ. IRISH WHISKEY

1 OZ. BAILEYS IRISH CREAM

1. Pour the coffee into a mug or Irish Coffee glass and add the sugar. Stir until the sugar has dissolved.

2. Add the whiskey and stir again. Top with Baileys Irish Cream. If you can, pour the Baileys over the back of a spoon to layer it on top rather than stirring it in.

MEXICAN HOT CHOCOLATE

6 OZ. WHOLE MILK

2 OZ. HALF-AND-HALF

3 CINNAMON STICKS

1 RED CHILI PEPPER, STEMMED
AND SEEDED

1 OZ. SWEETENED CONDENSED MILK

½ TEASPOON PURE VANILLA EXTRACT

1 TEASPOON FRESHLY GRATED
NUTMEG

½ TEASPOON FINE SEA SALT

1 OZ. TEQUILA

1 OZ. ABUELITA CHOCOLATE

WHIPPED CREAM, FOR GARNISH

1. Place the milk, half-and-half, cinnamon sticks, and chili pepper in a saucepan and warm the mixture over medium-low heat for 5 to 6 minutes, making sure it does not come to a boil. When the mixture starts to steam, remove the cinnamon sticks and chili pepper.

2. Add the sweetened condensed milk and whisk until combined. Stir in the vanilla, nutmeg, and salt.

3. Place the tequila and chocolate in a mug. Pour the warmed milk over them and stir until the chocolate has melted. Top with whipped cream and enjoy.

ELEVATED IRISH COFFEE

¾ OZ. BUSHMILLS BLACK BUSH IRISH WHISKEY

½ OZ. SIMPLE SYRUP

½ TEASPOON PEDRO XIMÉNEZ SHERRY

2 OZ. FRESHLY BREWED MEDIUM-ROAST ESPRESSO

HOT WATER, TO TOP

HEAVY CREAM, LIGHTLY WHIPPED, FOR GARNISH

1. Fill an Irish Coffee glass with boiling water. When the glass is warm, discard the water.

2. Add the whiskey, syrup, and sherry to the glass and stir to combine.

3. Add the espresso and hot water—reserving room for the cream—and stir to incorporate.

4. Float the cream on top by pouring it over the back of a spoon.

BABY
IT'S
YOU

6 OZ. FRESHLY BREWED COFFEE

2 OZ. MEZCAL

½ OZ. CINNAMON SYRUP
(SEE BELOW)

1 STRIP OF ORANGE PEEL,
FOR GARNISH

1. Place the coffee, mezcal, and syrup in a mug and stir to combine.

2. Garnish with the strip of orange peel and enjoy.

Cinnamon Syrup

Place 1 cup sugar and 1 cup water in a small saucepan and bring to a boil, stirring to dissolve the sugar. When the sugar has dissolved, add 3 cinnamon sticks, cook for another minute, and remove the pan from heat. Let it cool completely and strain before using.

CLASSICS

At any holiday gathering, there will always be a handful of guests who cruise right past whatever special serve you've crafted and instead want to celebrate with their favorite—a Martini, Old Fashioned, Margarita, or the like. These classic recipes make sure you can handle such requests with grace and warmth.

OLD
FASHIONED

1 TEASPOON CASTER SUGAR

2 TO 3 DASHES OF ANGOSTURA BITTERS

DASH OF WATER

2 OZ. BOURBON OR RYE WHISKEY

1 STRIP OF LEMON PEEL, FOR GARNISH

1 MARASCHINO CHERRY, FOR GARNISH

1. Place the sugar, bitters, and water in a double rocks glass and stir until the sugar has dissolved.

2. Add the whiskey and ice to the glass and stir until chilled. Express the strip of lemon peel over the cocktail, drop it into the glass, and garnish the cocktail with the maraschino cherry.

Caster Sugar

Caster sugar is a super-fine sugar with a consistency that sits somewhere between granulated and confectioners' sugar. Since it can dissolve without heat, unlike granulated sugar, it is tailor-made for cocktails. This ideal fit comes with a hefty price tag at the store, but you can easily make caster sugar at home with nothing more than a food processor or a blender and some granulated sugar. Place the granulated sugar in the food processor or blender and pulse until the consistency is super-fine, but short of powdery. Let the sugar settle in the food processor, transfer it to a container, and label to avoid future confusion.

MARTINI

3 OZ. LONDON DRY GIN

½ OZ. DRY VERMOUTH

1 LEMON TWIST, FOR GARNISH

1. Chill a cocktail glass in the freezer.

2. Place the gin and vermouth in a mixing glass, fill it two-thirds of the way with ice, and stir until chilled.

3. Strain into the chilled glass and garnish with a lemon twist.

MARGARITA

SALT, FOR THE RIM

2 OZ. TEQUILA

1 OZ. ORANGE LIQUEUR

1 OZ. FRESH LIME JUICE

1 LIME WHEEL, FOR GARNISH

1. Rim a coupe with the salt and, if desired, add ice to the glass.

2. Place the tequila, liqueur, and lime juice in a cocktail shaker, fill it two-thirds of the way with ice, and then shake vigorously until chilled.

3. Strain the cocktail into the glass and garnish with the lime wheel.

COSMOPOLITAN

1 OZ. VODKA

1 OZ. TRIPLE SEC

1½ OZ. CRANBERRY JUICE

½ OZ. FRESH LIME JUICE

1 LIME WHEEL, FOR GARNISH

1. Chill a cocktail glass in the freezer.

2. Place the vodka, triple sec, cranberry juice, and lime juice in a cocktail shaker, fill it two-thirds of the way with ice, and shake until chilled.

3. Strain into the chilled cocktail glass and garnish with the lime wheel.

GIN
& TONIC

2½ OZ. GIN

2½ OZ. TONIC WATER

SPLASH OF FRESH LIME JUICE

1 LIME WEDGE, FOR GARNISH

1. Fill a rocks glass with ice, add the gin and tonic water, and stir until chilled.

2. Top with the lime juice and garnish with the lime wedge.

NEGRONI

⅔ OZ. CAMPARI

⅔ OZ. SWEET VERMOUTH

2 OZ. GIN

1 ORANGE TWIST, FOR GARNISH

1. Place the Campari, sweet vermouth, and gin in a mixing glass, fill the glass two-thirds of the way with ice, and stir until chilled.

2. Strain the cocktail over ice into a rocks glass and garnish with the orange twist.

ESSENTIAL
BLOODY
MARY

1 TABLESPOON FRESH LEMON JUICE

1 TABLESPOON FRESH LIME JUICE

4 OZ. TOMATO JUICE

2 DASHES OF WORCESTERSHIRE SAUCE

PINCH OF SEA SALT

PINCH OF CELERY SALT

PINCH OF COARSELY GROUND BLACK PEPPER

¼ TEASPOON PEELED AND GRATED HORSERADISH

2 OZ. VODKA

1. Place all of the ingredients in a cocktail shaker, fill it two-thirds of the way with ice, and shake vigorously until chilled.

2. Strain into a pint glass filled with ice and garnish as desired.

DAIQUIRI

2 OZ. WHITE RUM

½ OZ. FRESH LIME JUICE

½ TEASPOON CASTER SUGAR

1 LIME WHEEL, FOR GARNISH

1. Chill a coupe in the freezer.

2. Add the rum, lime juice, and caster sugar to a cocktail shaker, fill it two-thirds of the way with ice, and shake until chilled.

3. Strain into the chilled coupe and garnish with the lime wheel.

MANHATTAN

2 OZ. RYE WHISKEY

⅔ OZ. SWEET VERMOUTH

2 DROPS OF AROMATIC BITTERS

1 MARASCHINO CHERRY, FOR GARNISH

1. Chill a cocktail glass in the freezer.

2. Place the whiskey, vermouth, and bitters in a mixing glass, fill it two-thirds of the way with ice, and stir until chilled.

3. Strain into the cocktail glass and garnish with the maraschino cherry.

MINT
JULEP

4 FRESH MINT LEAVES

1 TEASPOON CASTER SUGAR

SPLASH OF WATER

2 OZ. BOURBON

1 SPRIG OF FRESH MINT, FOR GARNISH

1. Place the mint leaves, sugar, and water in a rocks glass and muddle.

2. Fill the glass with crushed ice, add the bourbon, and stir until chilled.

3. Garnish with the sprig of mint.

VIEUX
CARRÉ

¾ OZ. RYE WHISKEY

¾ OZ. COGNAC

¾ OZ. SWEET VERMOUTH

1 BAR SPOON OF BÉNÉDICTINE

DASH OF PEYCHAUD'S BITTERS

DASH OF ANGOSTURA BITTERS

1 LEMON TWIST, FOR GARNISH

1. Place the rye, Cognac, vermouth, Bénédictine, and bitters in a mixing glass, fill it two-thirds of the way with ice, and stir until chilled.

2. Strain over one large ice cube into a rocks glass and garnish with the lemon twist.

ROB ROY

2 OZ. SCOTCH WHISKY

1 OZ. SWEET VERMOUTH

2 DROPS OF ANGOSTURA BITTERS

2 LUXARDO MARASCHINO CHERRIES,
FOR GARNISH

1. Add the Scotch, vermouth, and bitters to a mixing glass, fill it two-thirds of the way with ice, and stir until chilled.

2. Strain into a cocktail glass and garnish with the Luxardo maraschino cherries.

TOM
COLLINS

2 OZ. OLD TOM GIN

1 OZ. SIMPLE SYRUP

¾ OZ. FRESH LEMON JUICE

CLUB SODA, TO TOP

1 LEMON WHEEL, FOR GARNISH

1 MARASCHINO CHERRY, FOR GARNISH

1. Fill a Collins glass with ice and place it in the freezer.

2. Place the gin, syrup, and lemon juice in a cocktail shaker, fill it two-thirds of the way with ice, and shake until chilled.

3. Strain into the chilled Collins glass and top with the club soda.

4. Garnish with the lemon wheel and cherry.

BOULEVARDIER

1 OZ. BOURBON

1 OZ. CAMPARI

1 OZ. SWEET VERMOUTH

1 ORANGE TWIST, FOR GARNISH

1. Place the bourbon, Campari, and vermouth in a mixing glass, fill it two-thirds of the way with ice, and stir until chilled.

2. Strain over ice into a rocks glass and garnish with the orange twist.

AVIATION

2 OZ. LONDON DRY GIN

½ OZ. LUXARDO MARASCHINO
LIQUEUR

¼ OZ. CRÈME DE VIOLETTE

½ OZ. FRESH LEMON JUICE

1 MARASCHINO CHERRY,
FOR GARNISH

1. Chill a cocktail glass in the freezer.

2. Place the gin, Luxardo, crème de violette,
   and lemon juice in a cocktail shaker, fill it
   two-thirds of the way with ice, and shake
   until chilled.

3. Strain into the chilled glass and garnish with
   the cherry.

BEE'S
KNEES

2 OZ. DRY GIN

¾ OZ. FRESH LEMON JUICE

¾ OZ. HONEY SYRUP

SPRIG OF FRESH THYME,
FOR GARNISH

1. Chill a coupe in the freezer.

2. Place the gin, lemon juice, and honey syrup in a cocktail shaker, fill it two-thirds of the way with ice, and shake until chilled.

3. Strain into the chilled coupe and garnish with the sprig of thyme.

GIMLET

1½ OZ. GIN

½ OZ. FRESH LIME JUICE

1 LIME TWIST, FOR GARNISH

1. Place the gin and lime juice in a cocktail shaker, fill it two-thirds of the way with ice, and shake until chilled.

2. Strain into a cocktail glass and garnish with the lime twist.

DIRTY
MARTINI

3 OZ. GIN

¾ OZ. DRY VERMOUTH

SPLASH OF OLIVE BRINE

3 PIMENTO-STUFFED OLIVES,
FOR GARNISH

1. Place the gin, vermouth, and olive brine in a mixing glass, fill it two-thirds of the way with ice, and stir until chilled.

2. Strain into a cocktail glass and garnish with the olives skewered on a toothpick.

Swapping blue cheese–stuffed olives in for the garnish is a much-loved variation among Martini devotees.

JOY
DIVISION

2 OZ. LONDON DRY GIN

1 OZ. DRY VERMOUTH

½ OZ. TRIPLE SEC

3 DASHES OF ABSINTHE

1 LEMON TWIST, FOR GARNISH

1. Place the gin, vermouth, triple sec, and absinthe in a mixing glass, fill it two-thirds of the way with ice, and stir until chilled.

2. Strain into a coupe and garnish with the lemon twist.

WHITE
RUSSIAN

2 OZ. VODKA

1 OZ. KAHLÚA

HEAVY CREAM, TO TASTE

1. Place a few ice cubes in a rocks glass.

2. Add the vodka and Kahlúa and stir until chilled. Top with a generous splash of heavy cream and slowly stir until combined.

MOSCOW
MULE

4 FRESH MINT LEAVES

JUICE OF ½ LIME

2 OZ. VODKA

6 OZ. GINGER BEER

1 LIME WEDGE, FOR GARNISH

1. Place the mint leaves at the bottom of a copper mug, add the lime juice, and muddle.

2. Add crushed ice to the mug, add the vodka and ginger beer, and garnish with the lime wedge.

VESPER
MARTINI

3 OZ. GIN

1 OZ. VODKA

½ OZ. LILLET BLANC OR COCCHI AMERICANO

1 LEMON TWIST, FOR GARNISH

1. Chill a coupe in the freezer.

2. Add the gin, vodka, and Lillet or Cocchi Americano to a cocktail shaker, fill it two-thirds of the way with ice, and shake until chilled.

3. Strain into the chilled coupe and garnish with the lemon twist.

ESPRESSO
MARTINI

2 OZ. VODKA

1 OZ. FRESHLY BREWED ESPRESSO

½ OZ. KAHLÚA

3 ESPRESSO BEANS, FOR GARNISH

1. Chill a cocktail glass in the freezer.

2. Place the vodka, espresso, and Kahlúa in a cocktail shaker, fill it two-thirds of the way with ice, and shake until chilled.

3. Double-strain into the chilled glass and garnish with the espresso beans.

Even though it will cool in the shaker, be sure to use a steaming hot shot of espresso so that the cocktail retains the crema.

BRANDY
ALEXANDER

1½ OZ. BRANDY OR COGNAC

1 OZ. CRÈME DE CACAO

¾ OZ. HEAVY CREAM

FRESHLY GRATED NUTMEG,
FOR GARNISH

1. Chill a cocktail glass in the freezer.

2. Place the ingredients in a cocktail shaker, fill it two-thirds of the way with ice, and shake until chilled.

3. Strain into the chilled cocktail glass and garnish with the nutmeg.

MOJITO

8 FRESH MINT LEAVES

1 OZ. SIMPLE SYRUP

1 OZ. FRESH LIME JUICE

2 OZ. WHITE RUM

1 SPRIG OF FRESH MINT, FOR GARNISH

1. Place the mint leaves in the palm of one hand and slap them to activate their aroma. Place them in the bottom of a Collins glass and add the syrup and lime juice.

2. Fill the glass halfway with crushed ice. Gently stir until lightly chilled, about 10 seconds. Add the rum and more crushed ice and briefly stir to combine.

3. Fill the remainder of the glass with crushed ice and garnish with the sprig of mint.

SIDECAR

SUGAR, FOR THE RIM (OPTIONAL)

1½ OZ. COGNAC

¾ OZ. COINTREAU

¾ OZ. FRESH LEMON JUICE

1 LEMON TWIST, FOR GARNISH

1. If desired, rim a coupe with sugar.

2. Place the Cognac, Cointreau, and lemon juice in a cocktail shaker, fill it two-thirds of the way with ice, and shake until chilled.

3. Strain into the coupe and garnish with the lemon twist.

GRASSHOPPER

1 OZ. GREEN CRÈME DE MENTHE

1 OZ. WHITE CRÈME DE CACAO

1 OZ. HEAVY CREAM

1. Chill a cocktail glass in the freezer.

2. Place the ingredients in a cocktail shaker, fill it two-thirds of the way with ice, and shake until chilled.

3. Strain into the chilled glass.

SAZERAC

⅛ OZ. HERBSAINT

1 SUGAR CUBE

3 DASHES OF PEYCHAUD'S BITTERS

1½ OZ. SAZERAC RYE WHISKEY

1 LEMON TWIST, FOR GARNISH

1. Chill a rocks glass in the freezer.

2. Remove the glass from the freezer, add the Herbsaint, and rinse the glass with it. Discard any excess and set the glass aside.

3. Drop the sugar cube in a mixing glass, add the bitters, and muddle. Add the rye along with ice, stir until chilled, and strain the cocktail into the glass.

4. Garnish with the lemon twist.

SPARKLING
COCKTAILS

Nothing screams "Let's celebrate!" like
an effervescent, bubbly cocktail, those
bright-tasting serves that shimmer like
the lights on the tree and the stars in
the sky on those impossibly clear and
brutally cold winter nights. Whether
you're searching for that one last thing
to make your party perfect, or looking
to ring in the New Year with something
slightly more special than the traditional
bottle of bubbly, you're certain to find an
answer here.

MIMOSA

3 OZ. ORANGE JUICE

3 OZ. CHAMPAGNE

1. Place the orange juice in a champagne flute and top with the Champagne.

LOVE
& HAPPINESS

2 OZ. SINGLE-MALT WHISKY

1 OZ. AVERNA AMARO

2 OZ. DRY SPARKLING WINE

1. Chill a champagne flute in the freezer.

2. Place the whisky and amaro in a mixing glass, fill it two-thirds of the way with ice, and stir until chilled.

3. Strain into the chilled champagne flute and top with the sparkling wine.

FRENCH
75

1 SUGAR CUBE

JUICE OF 1 LEMON WEDGE

1 OZ. GIN

2 OZ. CHAMPAGNE

1 LEMON TWIST, FOR GARNISH

1 LUXARDO MARASCHINO CHERRY,
FOR GARNISH

1. Place the sugar cube in a champagne flute and add the lemon juice.

2. Add the gin and top with the Champagne.

3. Garnish the cocktail with the lemon twist. Skewer the cherry with a toothpick, place it over the mouth of the champagne flute, and enjoy.

A SILVER SONG

1 OZ. OLD TOM GIN

½ OZ. FRESH LEMON JUICE

½ OZ. SIMPLE SYRUP

CHAMPAGNE, TO TOP

1 LEMON TWIST, FOR GARNISH

1. Place the gin, lemon juice, and syrup in a cocktail shaker, fill it two-thirds of the way with ice, and shake until chilled.

2. Strain into a champagne flute, top with the Champagne, and garnish with the lemon twist.

UNLIKELY
ALLIES

1 OZ. TEQUILA

1 OZ. GRAPEFRUIT SODA

2 OZ. CHAMPAGNE

1. Place the tequila and soda in a champagne flute and gently swirl to combine.

2. Top with the Champagne and enjoy.

IT WAS A
VERY GOOD
YEAR

FLEUR DE SEL, FOR THE RIM

2 OZ. PREMIUM TEQUILA

1 OZ. GRAND MARNIER

1 OZ. FRESH LIME JUICE

4 OZ. CHAMPAGNE

1 LIME TWIST, FOR GARNISH

1. Rim a rocks glass with the fleur de sel and add ice to the glass.

2. Place the tequila, Grand Marnier, and lime juice in a cocktail shaker, fill it two-thirds of the way with ice, and shake until chilled.

3. Strain into the rocks glass, top with the Champagne, and garnish with the lime twist.

YOU SERIOUS, CLARK?

1 OZ. PEACH VODKA (SEE BELOW)

1 OZ. CRANBERRY JUICE

SPARKLING WINE, TO TOP

1 LEMON TWIST, FOR GARNISH

1. Place the vodka and cranberry juice in a mixing glass, add ice, and stir until chilled.

2. Strain into a champagne flute, top with sparkling wine, and garnish with the lemon twist.

Peach Vodka

Place three halved peaches and a 750 ml bottle of vodka in a mason jar, cover, and store in a cool dark place for 48 minutes. Strain before using or storing.

BELLINI

2 OZ. PEACH NECTAR

¼ OZ. FRESH LEMON JUICE

CHAMPAGNE, TO TOP

1. Place the peach nectar and lemon juice in a cocktail shaker, fill it two-thirds of the way with ice, and shake until chilled.

2. Strain into a champagne flute and top with Champagne.

LIPSTICK
& ROUGE

¾ OZ. APEROL

¾ OZ. AMARETTO

¾ OZ. FRESH LEMON JUICE

3 OZ. PROSECCO

1 LEMON TWIST, FOR GARNISH

1. Place the Aperol, amaretto, and lemon juice in a cocktail shaker, fill it two-thirds of the way with ice, and shake until chilled.

2. Strain into a champagne flute, top with the Prosecco, and garnish with the lemon twist.

HEADLIGHTS LOOK LIKE DIAMONDS

½ OZ. ST-GERMAIN

1 OZ. GIFFARD CRÈME DE PAMPLEMOUSSE ROSE

CHAMPAGNE, TO TOP

1 GRAPEFRUIT TWIST, FOR GARNISH

1. Pour the liqueurs into a champagne flute, top with Champagne, and garnish with the grapefruit twist.

DREAMFLOWER

1 OZ. WHISKEY

2 OZ. APPLE CIDER

2 OZ. HARD SPARKLING CIDER

1. Place the whiskey and apple cider in a rocks glass, add ice as desired, and gently stir until chilled.

2. Top with the sparkling cider and enjoy.

A CERTAIN RATIO

- 1 OZ. PIMM'S NO. 1
- ¾ OZ. PISCO
- ¾ OZ. THAI BASIL & STRAWBERRY SHRUB (SEE BELOW)
- ¼ OZ. FRESH LEMON JUICE
- 2 OZ. SPARKLING WINE
- 1 LEMON TWIST, FOR GARNISH

1. Place the Pimm's, pisco, shrub, and lemon juice in a cocktail shaker, fill it two-thirds of the way with ice, and shake until chilled.

2. Strain over ice into a wine glass, top with the sparkling wine, and garnish with the lemon twist.

Thai Basil & Strawberry Shrub

Place 2 lbs. strawberries, 8 cups sugar, 8 cups water, and 1 cup of firmly packed Thai basil leaves in a large saucepan. Bring to a boil over medium-high heat and cook until the mixture has reduced by one-quarter, stirring to dissolve the sugar. Turn off the heat and let the mixture cool to room temperature. Strain through a fine sieve into a large bowl and stir in 2 cups of rice vinegar.

THE ROSE PARADE

3 OZ. RED WINE

1 OZ. STRAWBERRY & GIN REDUCTION (SEE BELOW)

3 OZ. CHAMPAGNE

2 STRAWBERRIES, FOR GARNISH

1. Place the wine and reduction in a wine glass and stir to combine.

2. Top with the Champagne, garnish with the strawberries, and enjoy.

Strawberry & Gin Reduction

Place 2 oz. gin and 4 strawberries in a food processor and puree until smooth. Strain into a small saucepan and cook over medium heat until the mixture has reduced by half. Let cool completely before using.

BLACK
VELVET

5 OZ. CHAMPAGNE

5 OZ. STOUT

1. Pour the champagne into a mason jar or pint glass.

2. Carefully pour the stout over the back of a spoon to layer it on top of the Champagne.

I FEEL IT STARTS AGAIN

1 OZ. COINTREAU

1 OZ. BRANDY

3 OZ. CHAMPAGNE

1. Place the Cointreau and brandy in a cocktail shaker, fill it two-thirds of the way with ice, and shake until chilled.

2. Strain into a champagne flute and top with the Champagne.

LEMON
FIZZ

½ OZ. GIN

⅓ OZ. FRESH LEMON JUICE

PINCH OF CASTER SUGAR

3 OZ. CHAMPAGNE

1 LEMON TWIST, FOR GARNISH

1. Place the gin, lemon juice, and caster sugar in a cocktail shaker, fill it two-thirds of the way with ice, and shake until chilled.

2. Strain into a champagne flute, top with the Champagne, and garnish with the lemon twist.

IT'S THE SPIRIT OF THE SEASON

The holidays are a chance to see loved ones and reconnect with old friends, to revive ancient traditions and establish new ones. These playful, refreshing, and holiday-themed cocktails are ready to inject themselves into any of those happenings and enliven them. Whether you're settling in with a favorite holiday flick or trying to keep the merriment going in the lull between opening presents and Christmas dinner, these festive drinks will help make the moment memorable.

CHRISTMAPOLITAN

1½ OZ. VODKA

1 OZ. ST-GERMAIN

1 OZ. CRANBERRY SAUCE

½ OZ. FRESH LIME JUICE

2 DASHES OF FIG BITTERS

1. Chill a cocktail glass in the freezer.

2. Place all of the ingredients in a cocktail shaker, fill it two-thirds of the way with ice, and shake until chilled.

3. Strain into the chilled glass.

AN ANGEL GETS HIS WINGS

SALT, FOR THE RIM

1 OZ. FRESH LIME JUICE

2 OZ. TEQUILA

1 OZ. ORANGE LIQUEUR

2 OZ. CRANBERRY JUICE

1 LIME TWIST, FOR GARNISH

HANDFUL OF CRANBERRIES, FOR GARNISH

1. Wet the rim of a coupe and coat it with the salt.

2. Place all of the remaining ingredients, except for the garnishes, in a cocktail shaker, fill it two-thirds of the way with ice, and shake until chilled.

3. Strain the cocktail into the rimmed coupe and garnish with the lime twist and handful of cranberries.

CHRISTMAS TIME IS HERE

CANDY CANE CRUMBLES, FOR THE RIM

2 OZ. GIN

⅔ OZ. DRY VERMOUTH

⅔ OZ. PEPPERMINT SCHNAPPS

1 PEPPERMINT, FOR GARNISH

1. Wet the rim of a cocktail glass and then dip it into the crumbled candy cane.

2. Place the gin, vermouth, and schnapps in a mixing glass, fill it two-thirds of the way with ice, and stir until chilled.

3. Strain the contents of the cocktail shaker into the cocktail glass and garnish with a peppermint.

SNOW
BOWL

2 OZ. GIN

2 OZ. WHITE CHOCOLATE LIQUEUR

SPLASH OF WHITE CRÈME DE MENTHE

FRESHLY GRATED NUTMEG, FOR
GARNISH

1. Place the gin, liqueur, and crème de menthe in a cocktail shaker, fill it two-thirds of the way with ice, and shake until chilled.

2. Strain over ice into a rocks glass and garnish with a dusting of nutmeg.

BY THE CHIMNEY WITH CARE

2 OZ. TEQUILA

1 OZ. HEAVY CREAM

1 OZ. CRÈME DE CACAO

1 TEASPOON CHAMBORD

1. Chill a coupe in the freezer.

2. Place the ingredients in a cocktail shaker, fill it two-thirds of the way with ice, and shake until chilled.

3. Strain into the chilled coupe.

SON OF A
NUTCRACKER

2 OZ. WHISKEY

¾ OZ. ROSEMARY SYRUP
(SEE PAGE 31)

SELTZER WATER, TO TOP

1 SPRIG OF FRESH ROSEMARY,
FOR GARNISH

1 GRAPEFRUIT WEDGE, FOR GARNISH

1. Place the whiskey and syrup in a tumbler
   filled with ice and stir until chilled.

2. Top with the seltzer and garnish with the sprig
   of rosemary and grapefruit wedge.

BLUE
CHRISTMAS

1½ OZ. VODKA

1½ OZ. BLUE CURAÇAO

1 OZ. FRESH LEMON JUICE

DASH OF FRESH LIME JUICE

1 LEMON SLICE, FOR GARNISH

1. Place the vodka, blue Curaçao, and lemon juice in a cocktail shaker, fill it two-thirds of the way with ice, and shake until chilled.

2. Strain over ice into a rocks glass and top with the lime juice. Gently stir to combine.

3. Garnish with the slice of lemon.

A PARROT IN A PALM TREE

1½ OZ. REPOSADO TEQUILA

½ OZ. MEZCAL

½ OZ. ORANGE LIQUEUR

2 OZ. SPICED COCONUT SYRUP
(SEE BELOW)

1 OZ. FRESH LIME JUICE

1 LEMON WHEEL, FOR GARNISH

1. Place all of the ingredients, except for the lemon wheel, in a cocktail shaker, fill it two-thirds of the way with ice, and shake until chilled.

2. Strain over ice into a Collins glass and garnish with the lemon wheel.

Spiced Coconut Syrup

Place 1 cup coconut water, 1 cup demerara sugar, 3 cinnamon sticks, 5 cloves, 5 allspice berries, and 3 cardamom pods in a saucepan. Cook over low heat, stirring until the sugar has dissolved and the mixture is thick enough to coat the back of a wooden spoon. Remove the pan from heat, let cool completely, and strain before using.

FELIZ
NAVIDAD

2 OZ. CHIPOTLE RUM (SEE BELOW)

1 OZ. CREAM OF COCONUT

1 OZ. ORANGE JUICE

4 OZ. PINEAPPLE JUICE

FRESHLY GRATED NUTMEG,
FOR GARNISH

1 ORANGE SLICE, FOR GARNISH

1. Place the rum, cream of coconut, orange juice, and pineapple juice in a cocktail shaker, fill it two-thirds of the way with crushed ice, and shake until chilled.

2. Pour the contents of the shaker into a glass, grate nutmeg over the cocktail, and garnish with the orange slice.

Chipotle Rum

Place 1 cup aged rum and 1 torn dried chipotle pepper in a mason jar and let the mixture steep at room temperature for 3 hours. Strain and use as desired.

THREE
WISE
MEN

½ OZ. JIM BEAM BOURBON

½ OZ. JACK DANIEL'S TENNESSEE WHISKEY

½ OZ. JOHNNIE WALKER SCOTCH WHISKY

1. Place the ingredients in a cocktail shaker, fill it two-thirds of the way with ice, and shake until chilled.

2. Strain over ice into a rocks glass and enjoy.

SANTA'S
SUIT

SUGAR, FOR THE RIM

½ OZ. COINTREAU

½ OZ. CHAMBORD

½ OZ. CRANBERRY JUICE

1. Place the ingredients in a mixing glass, fill it two-thirds of the way with ice, and stir until chilled.

2. Strain into a coupe and enjoy.

TEN GRINCHES, PLUS TWO

1 TEASPOON CINNAMON WATER
(SEE BELOW)

1½ OZ. QUALITY VODKA

1 OZ. FRESH LIME JUICE

1 OZ. FRESH ORANGE JUICE

¼ OZ. GRAND MARNIER

CINNAMON, FOR GARNISH (OPTIONAL)

1. Place all of the ingredients, except for the cinnamon, in a cocktail shaker, fill it two-thirds of the way with ice, and shake until chilled.

2. Strain into a cocktail glass and garnish with the dusting of cinnamon, if desired.

Cinnamon Water

Combine a cinnamon stick, 1 teaspoon sugar, and 1 cup boiling water and steep for 30 minutes. Discard the cinnamon stick before using.

METRIC
CONVERSIONS

US Measurement	Approximate Metric Liquid Measurement	Approximate Metric Dry Measurement
1 TEASPOON	5 ML	5 G
1 TABLESPOON OR ½ OUNCE	15 ML	14 G
1 OUNCE OR ⅛ CUP	30 ML	29 G
¼ CUP OR 2 OUNCES	60 ML	57 G
⅓ CUP	80 ML	76 G
½ CUP OR 4 OUNCES	120 ML	113 G
⅔ CUP	160 ML	151 G
¾ CUP OR 6 OUNCES	180 ML	170 G
1 CUP OR 8 OUNCES OR ½ PINT	240 ML	227 G
1½ CUPS OR 12 OUNCES	350 ML	340 G
2 CUPS OR 1 PINT OR 16 OUNCES	475 ML	454 G
3 CUPS OR 1½ PINTS	700 ML	680 G
4 CUPS OR 2 PINTS OR 1 QUART	950 ML	908 G

INDEX

ABOUT CIDER MILL PRESS BOOK PUBLISHERS

Good ideas ripen with time. From seed to harvest, Cider Mill Press brings fine reading, information, and entertainment together between the covers of its creatively crafted books. Our Cider Mill bears fruit twice a year, publishing a new crop of titles each spring and fall.

"Where Good Books Are Ready for Press"

Visit us online at
cidermillpress.com
or write to us at
PO Box 454
12 Spring St.
Kennebunkport, Maine 04046